High Octane Leadership

Pole Position Performance

Biagio "Bill" Sciacca

Pole
Position
Performance

B iagio "Bill" Sciacca spent his formative years in the town of Pittston, PA., a small coal mining town in North East Pennsylvania.

He is the owner of Intelligent Motivation Inc., **www.intelligentmotivationinc.com**, an award winning, global consulting and training firm specializing in management consulting, leadership training, and psychological assessment for hiring and staff development.

Bill earned his MBA and PhD. in Business Administration, as well as his bachelor's degree in Philosophy and Sociology. He is the author of several books relating to goal setting. His upcoming book, *Provocative Leadership*, will be published soon. Provocative Leadership is based upon the philosophical underpinnings of leadership and how to apply the concepts to your own personal leadership style.

A dynamic speaker, executive leader, as well as a gifted teacher,

Bill takes great pleasure in preparing people to become more successful. Since 1993, he has motivated more than 30,000 people. Now residing in Tamarindo, Costa Rica, he divides his time between his international clients and writing his next book.

Bill's greatest passion is to assist organizations in motivating their employees to own their company's mission and goals. A highly sought-after trainer, Bill's presentations are informative and inter-active with consistent and company–wide measurable results.

His company Intelligent Motivation, Inc. is designed to offer highly enlightened, moti-vational material in a well-researched and documented form thus bridging the gap between academic theory and practical application.

Intro
duction

It's funny how this writing thing works out. *Provocative Leadership* is finished and is ready to go into publication. I'm happy with the overall structure of the work, but it seemed as if there should've been a step before provocative leadership.

I spent a great deal of my day thinking about the behaviors that leaders exhibit and how they can enhance their performance by changing some behaviors and adding new behaviors.

I was taking a break from my mental cogitation, went to Facebook, just to clear my head, and there was a picture of a drag race car on the screen. I thought that the fuel for that car must be so enormously high-octane that it produces gigantic speed in a short period of time.

Bam! That was what I was looking for to introduce *Provocative Leadership*.

As *High-Octane Leadership* began to take on a life of its own, I realized that this book lent itself very well to a short webinar. Consequently, a webinar and this e-book have been combined to give the readers a one – two punch as to developing leadership behaviors.

As the webinar developed along with the book it occurred to me that personal leadership, the art and practice of dynamic goalsetting and other attributes of self–development should be looked at also.

Thus, a 14-week program entitled *Dynamics of Personal Leadership* was born, also as a result of High-Octane Leadership. This is a continuous process which is evolving into assisting as many people as possible. And it warms my heart to be able to do just that.

Whether you decide to invest in any of my other processes that is completely up to you. I am of an age and income bracket of not having to earn a living by doing this. I do is because I want to and because I love to!

One other thing you will notice in *High-Octane Leadership*, revolving around this whole racecar thing, is at the end of every chapter there is a bonus. A little blurb that really has nothing to do with the chapter content just a little addition for you to think about. They are called additives. Just like you would put into an automobile to increase the octane to increase performance.

That was a bit of an afterthought, but I hope you will write to me to let me know whe-ther they were a good addition, or if each of the seven additives should be a book in itself.

At some point you have to stop. Because, if you don't the work will never get into the hands of the reader. So, I stopped! Here it is!

I hope you enjoy reading as much as I did writing.

Like I said, it's funny how this writing thing works!

Pre
face

When the best leader's work is done the people say, "We did it ourselves." -Lau Tzu

"I would say that the quality of each man's life is the full measure of that man's personal commitment to excellence and to victory—whether it be football, whether it be business, whether it be politics or government…" The key word here is personal. High-octane leaders are personally invested, confident, happy, and fully engaged individuals. Before they inherit the position or title, at their core, these attributes personify who they are on a daily and consistent basis. Whether they are in the workplace, on the field, or at home, you will find them demonstrating these characteristics. High–octane leadership can be observed in the workplace, playing with children, singing in a choir, or on the golf course.

What are high-octane leaders? They are the distinguishing force between a good orga-nization and an excellent organization. They are the engines of an organization, and in the same way that an engine in an automobile must be taken care of, a leader must receive the appropriate care and maintenance to function at the highest capacity. This book offers a dynamic and effective approach to boosting your octane for maximum leadership performance. It also offers additives that will keep you performing at your optimum level. If you are ready to become a high-octane leader who is well-equipped to lead, influence, inspire, and focus on your goals, then let's get started!

By the way, if you are not a giant racecar fan, and you may be wondering why I used the subheading pole position performance, here's a definition of Pole Position Performance:

In motorsports the pole position is the position at the inside of the front row at the start of a racing event. This position is typically given to the vehicle and driver with the best qualifying time in the trials before the race (the leader in the starting grid).

What I love about the title high-octane leadership, and the subheading Pole Position Performance is two-fold: one, is the depiction of leadership skills as a behavioral engine. The better the fuel you feed the engine the greater the performance. Two, the pole position, which is the best position to start a race normally goes to the person who has won the pre-qualifier. Thus, the better position to win already goes to the winner!

In a straightforward, easy-to-follow way, this book will help you:

1. Rate your performance
2. Develop self-awareness
3. Evaluate your habits

4. Increase your performance
5. Prepare for the unpredictable
6. Be teachable
7. Become an Inspiration

Stop for a moment. Look at the 7 attributes listed above and answer the following questions:

1. Which 3 are most important to you?
2. Can you rank them in order of importance?

What you have just accomplished is that you have developed a road map to guide you on your way!

Good luck on your journey!

Leadership
It's Personal

One of the widely-agreed-upon characteristics of high-octane leaders is that they are driven by intrinsic motivators—their output is abundant and consistent regardless of the reward. Oftentimes their performance is linked to the sheer fulfillment of the work they do and the relationships they form. Hold it! Does this mean that individuals who have acquired high-octane leadership behaviors are actually having fun at work? You bet! As a result, they are admired by their peers. People are receptive to their ideas and want to follow them. Can you think of a high-octane leader you'd love to follow? Better question, are you ready to become a leader whom people love to follow? You're on your way. Keep reading.

It's personal—high-octane leaders have a future-focused outlook. They are always considering where they are and where they desire to be and what they desire to do. While they engage substantial and intense mental application to their "right now" projects, high-octane leaders forecast for long-term and predictable success.

It's personal—high-octane leaders are superior self-motivators. Because they thrive on achieving, caring for others, and value how they show up in the world, they have a keen knack for digging deep within themselves to create the mental and physical energy for high-octane output. Creating a habit of self-motivation is paramount to high-octane leadership.

It's personal – it's all personal. The way we extend ourselves to others is personal. High-octane leadership is designed around personal and selfless giving.

Chapter 1
Mental Application
Must Be Consistent

"I have been impressed with the urgency of doing. Knowing is not enough; We must apply. Being willing is not enough; We must do." – Leonardo Da Vinci

Have you ever worked for an organization where the leader invested 80% of their time in only one or two departments? Perhaps the departments were revenue-producing areas of the organization, or their function related mostly to the leader's own strengths and interest. Regardless of the reason, inconsistent mental application breeds mistrust and low work performance.

Leaders must engage all levels of their organization with a consistent mental application. How is this consistent mental application demonstrated? By communicating genuine interest and concern in every team with the primary goal to make the organization a complete and fully functional entity. It requires focusing on the task at hand.

High-octane leaders realize the value and importance of understanding the organizations they influence and lead. Sure, they may not have a thorough knowledge of the day-to-day inner workings of each department, but they must apply the same care and concern to back-end support roles as they do with high-performing front-end positions. When we consider the bottom line, all departments are necessary to collectively drive a company's revenue and reputation.

DISCIPLINE FOR MENTAL APPLICATION

Someone wrote that it is possible to form a habit in only 21 days. If you recite The Gettysburg Address for 21 days, it is yours! However, rather than exercising our minds, we tend to invest much of our habit-forming energies on tangible patterns, such as going to the gym once a week, eating less at dinner, or setting an earlier bedtime. While those are excellent physical habits, mental discipline trumps physical discipline any day. Why? The seed of every action is a thought. If you can master your thinking in the area of food, for example, you can control your eating portions and consequently, your weight. Basically, physical habits began as an idea! Thus, what we manifest is what we think of most!

High-octane leaders become great leaders because they have disciplined their thoughts, which in turn impact their actions. You can create a competitive edge by forming habits that boost your mental application. Some positive habits are: Start your day in quiet meditation; practice positive affirmations; prioritize your day and read quality material that feeds your brain and attitude. We are bombarded daily with mental interruptions from every angle. Our cell phones, the television, the doorbell, and the environment in general interferes and hinders our thought processes. High-octane leaders understand the value of creating uninterrupted space for the mental downloads necessary to function at their highest mental capacity.

ROUTINE MAINTENANCE—PERSONAL GROWTH

If you look at the heavy hitters in leadership—Pacesetters like Warren Buffett, Ursula Burns, Jeff Bezos, Mary Barra, Jack Welch, and others, you should know they did not become great leaders by consulting only their own self-preserving principles. Whether directly or indirectly, they reference the leadership models, ideas, and feedback from other leaders, philosophers, and innovators. Some have business mentors that they consult periodically. Others hone their leadership skills within small networks. The point here is that you, too, must make the necessary "pit stops" to refuel, refresh and receive new insight to effectively lead with the appropriate leadership tools.

Don't hesitate to consult your peers to see what's working for them in their organizations and which ideas you might use within your corporate structure. Ideas are meant to be shared, and there are no rules against sharing models that work. Someone had to be first, but we can all benefit from the original blueprint and tweak it as we see fit.

In the same way that your vehicle has a maintenance timeline for things like tire rotation, oil change, filter change, and other vital upkeep and repair cycles, it's a good practice to create a leadership maintenance checklist in order to remain competitive and performing at your highest leadership capacity.

Once upon a time "burning the midnight oil" was favored, suggested and seen as a desirable trait of good leaders. We have since learned the value and necessity of getting proper rest to foster high-performance. In order for high-octane leaders to remain mentally invested, proper rest is essential. Many high-performing leaders have left their post and not merely because they grew weary. They became ill as a result of neglecting their health. High-octane leaders understand the value of taking a break from the race in order to engage mental application.

CHECK YOUR HAT AT THE DOOR
NOT YOUR HEART

High-octane leaders engage IQ and EQ to solve organizational challenges. Why? Because businesses aren't made up of facts and figures alone. People are included in the business equation. Unlike robots, people have feelings. Their input must be welcomed and valued. As it is with any relationship, communication is a driver of trust, longevity, and performance. When employees are encouraged to offer suggestions and take part in moving the company forward, you can count on their engagement, trust, and commitment. But, if they feel devalued, trust diminishes, and performance and morale will take a dive.

MANAGING VS. LEADING

High-octane leaders understand the stark differences between managing and leading. This area has been beaten to death in leadership literature and while it deserves some explanation I invite the reader to thwart the extensive differences between management and leadership in their own time.

Managing is heavily tied to processes, budgeting, planning, problem-solving and controlling human capital. Leadership is about giving others control—empowering them to lead. Leadership is about creating a vision with strategies and then engaging and influencing people to rally around the vision and bring it to fruition.

Are you leading or managing? Leading is working smart. Managing is working hard and working others even harder. On which side of this chart do you fall?

LEADERS	MANAGERS
Take risks and learn from their failures	Avoid taking risks
Forecast for future success	Focus on the short game
Expand their knowledge base continuously	Comfortable with and lean on past achievements
Build relationships with others	Build systems to bridge relationships
Coach others	Assign tasks

One of the primary differences between managers and leaders is very significant – Managers create followers. Leaders create leaders. High-octane leaders listen to their people and energize them to lead.

An employee in one department should always feel assured the leader is concerned about that particular department and about each individual's efforts. Employees want to know they are making an impact on the growth and stability of the company, and they need to hear it regularly.

This is not to say that management does not have a purpose or fine attributes associated with it. Keep in mind this book is not entitled high-octane management!

High-octane leaders provide consistent feedback and encouragement to everyone in their organization. David Johnson

Oragui, the founder and CEO of The Balanced Life Academy says it simply: "Consistency is the key to success."

Mental Application is a guiding-principle of high-octane leadership. Are you ready to get off the ledge and create a competitive edge? Continue on to chapter two.

ADDITIVE #1
WHAT GETS YOUR MOTOR RUNNING?

"Why lead?" is the first question a potential leader must answer. Your answer will determine how well you embrace the role of a leader. General William Tecumseh Sherman, a dynamic leader in the American Civil War, was urged to run in the Presidential race of 1884. Although his original statement regarding the election was much longer, historians have reduced it to these words, "If drafted, I will not run; if nominated, I will not accept; if elected, I will not serve." This is a straightforward example of rejecting a leadership role. Conversely, Ronald Reagan said, "The greatest leader is not necessarily the one who does the greatest things. He is the one that gets the people to do the greatest things." Therefore, you must ask yourself if you are up to the challenge of being a high-octane leader.

1. What drives you to lead?
2. Are you engaging in all levels of your organization?
3. Is your mental discipline greater than your physical discipline?
4. Are you forming positive habits for a high-octane leader?
5. Do you consult leaders that you admire for leadership advice?
6. Are you staying healthy or are you burning the midnight oil?
7. Do you see yourself as a manager or a leader?

"Intensity is the price of excellence" – Warren Buffett

Just as hardened build-up will slow down your car's performance, distractions can have the same effect on you. Learning ways to simplify your life will help you become a more efficient leader. You could start by removing the clutter from your mind. This will give you a clear focus, free from the distractions that slow you down. Studies show that the peak times for distractions at work are from 12 p.m. to 4 p.m. with 2 p.m. being the time when most people crash. High-octane leaders keep their focus on the tasks at hand and move seamlessly from one to the other, keeping interruptions to a minimum.

Many years ago, I was a writer for a magazine and I missed the deadline in submitting an article. Actually, I didn't miss the deadline – the editor typed the incorrect due date on the email which was a week after the real deadline. Since I was punctual and usually early with my submissions, he called me expressing his concern about the missing article on the day the it was due. I explained to him that he was a week early. After checking his email, he explained that he had mistakenly typed the wrong due date. It was 8:30 a.m. and the deadline was noon that day. He asked if I could finish what I had started and get it to him by noon anyway. I told him that a good amount of research was done – which it wasn't – and that I could get a section of it to him by the deadline. I told him that because I felt so bad about his plight. I spent the next several hours in intense research and writing; finishing the entire article. He emailed me afterwards and asked me how much of it had been completed prior to his call, since it was very well-written. I told him not to worry about my bag of tricks, but to worry about getting the dates correct in his future emails!

Although you may not have the experience I had in completing a task at that level of intensity, here are some ways to stay focused and increase your productivity. You never know when you will be painted into a corner, and the only way out is through the door you create in the wall.

Chapter 2
Intensity Is
A Choice

Block out Distractions – You are diligently working on a project and you hear a beep coming from your cell phone. Do you check to see what or who it is? If you answered yes, you are prone to distractions. It is hard to completely remove the temptation of your phone; therefore, blocking off a period of time to catch up on emails, social media posts, etc. could save you almost 5 hours of productivity in your work week. So, silence that ringer and turn off your notifications that do not require immediate action. You will see a huge difference in no time.

How do you block out distractions?

_____

Stop Multitasking – Studies have shown that multitasking lowers the IQ ten points. In a meeting full of professionals, there are usually several attendees who are checking their phones or reading material other than what the speaker is presenting. They have just lowered their IQ to that of an eight-year-old child! Another downside to multitasking is that you end up making mistakes. The most effective way to keep from making needless mistakes is to dedicate chunks of time to a certain task. Make a list of your daily routine and break up your tasks so that each one takes 20 to 30 minutes; then you can move on to the next one. You will be a better time manager and you will make fewer mistakes.

How to you stop yourself from multitasking?

Get Organized – This is easier said than done for some people, but you can start by putting your tasks in one place where you can see them all at a glance. By staying organized, you will save time knowing where everything is located and will have more time to work on the most important tasks. When items are organized and labeled neatly, tracking them down should be a walk in the park, rather than a source of stress! Using calendar alerts will ensure that you never miss a deadline again – sometimes allowing you to complete tasks early and impressing those around you.

How will you get organized?

Use Coping Strategies – Whenever you walk into a co-worker's office, you may notice that they have a desk toy or two. These toys are gifts that are marketed as "stress busters." A few years ago, it was discovered that using toys to lower stress and cope with anxiety enables workers to accomplish more in a day. If you have ever clicked a ballpoint pen over and over again, you are using a coping strategy. New theories suggest that items which someone might call distractions may actually be an ingenious way to "distract" the physical part of the brain. Playing with gadgets can release the workers' built-up anxieties and help them concentrate on the work at hand. A few examples of these items are: fidget spinners, stress balls, soft footballs, baseballs, and chewing gum.

What coping strategies do you use?

_____

Take Strategic Breaks – Have you ever been perplexed by a problem and then, after a short break, the answer suddenly comes to you? It is important to have short distractions but not constant mini-distractions. Taking a strategic break allows your brain the respite it needs to give you a fresh start. These necessary breaks also energize you and restore motivation which affects your decision-making. Studies have shown that a brief rest period allows the brain the time it needs to assimilate new information that it has been given. Short breaks also help you to stay better focused on your daily tasks.

When are your strategic breaks?

_____

Prior Planning – Most people begin planning their day immediately after arriving at the workplace. What if you did your daily planning the evening before your work day? It may sound unusual, but it actually helps you to be more productive. At the end of each day, write down the five to ten most important things you want to accomplish the next day. Start each day completing those items on your list.

Most people have a limited amount of willpower each day; therefore, by planning your days the night before, you are reserving your willpower for your most important work. You will also be surprised by how much your productivity will increase in less time than it did when you did no prior planning. A much-used catchphrase is: "Prior planning prevents poor performance."

What are your 3 most important items to accomplish tomorrow?

1._____,

2._____,

3._____,

MICROMANAGING VS. RELAXED INTENSITY

Micromanagement: Everyone knows the meaning of this term, and those who have experienced it often despise it. Micromanagement is frequently the top complaint people have about their employers. When the unemployment rate is low, this presents even more of a problem for companies. There are other significant issues with micromanagement; here are a few of the plethora of risks that come with this style of management:

- There is a breakdown in trust.
- Loss of creativity – Co-workers lose their incentive to be creative. The job where they desired to let their talents shine quickly loses its luster.
- Mental and physical health suffer.
- An employee or team can never reach their full potential.

High-octane leaders are the exact opposite of micromanagers. Leaders are pacesetters; they present new and unique ideas to the company in order to increase morale and create a definitive destination to reach. Once their goal is reached, it is the task of the leader to set a new standard and encourage the employees to pursue the current target. Leaders create an atmosphere where attrition is low because the workplace is a comfortable place.

Intensity is not only about focus but also about being relaxed. It has been said that the key to success in business and in life is relaxed intensity. Even though it is an oxymoron, it works. A leader who has relaxed intensity is a person who is calm through a trial and can maintain their composure through the most challenging times. They do not lose their cool. We all want the surgeon who has relaxed intensity – he is calm, cool and collected. His hands are steady while his eyes are intensely focused on the task at hand. In the same way, those who have fought in a war and have been fired upon will tell you that because they kept their composure, they were able to do what it took to stay alive. Soldiers who lose their heads are likely to lose their lives.

FORM A PERSONAL MISSION STATEMENT

In order to successfully lead others you must first know where you are going. A clearly defined personal mission statement will give you that direction. Without it, you will find yourself half committed to your organization and unable to fully support its mission. Having a Personal Mission Statement (PMS) gives you clarity of your purpose as an individual and a leader. If you don't know where you are going and aren't clear on your "why", how can you effectively lead an organization? In relation to focus, having your PMS integrated into your weekly planning schedule keeps it front and center.

If you haven't created one, there is no better time than the present. Personal mission statements are important components of leadership and personal development. They are somewhat different from a company mission statement, but the basic principles are the same. By focusing on the successes, you have had in the past, you can pinpoint what is important to you, which will help you identify your core values. Try to narrow down your core values until you are able to choose the one that best defines you. Use that knowledge to discover the ways you can make a difference in your job as well as your family and community. What is your "personal mission statement?"

PERSEVERANCE

Overcomers who beat the odds despite childhood upbringing and frequent failures point to a powerful trait: Perseverance. It is the key to winning. High-octane leaders have perseverance. They do not give in or give up in spite of difficulties, obstacles or discouragement. It is more important than skill or past experience.

Perseverance can be developed from within. It comes from a spirit that refuses to accept failure or the option of quitting. A leader who perseveres stands ready to endure for the long haul.

Leaders with perseverance strive to excel. They derive satisfaction from being unsatisfied. Dogged leaders continually measure how far they're willing to push themselves by how fervently they want to win.

ADDITIVE #2
COURAGE AND PERSEVERANCE

When it comes to perseverance, Winston Churchill was the quintessential persistent leader. During World War II, he was called upon to give a graduation speech at Harrow School, an all-boys boarding school he had attended in London. If you want a blueprint for the perseverance of a high-octane leader, you will find it in his remarks on Oct 29, 1941. They not only encouraged an entire country but also the entire world. Many leaders still refer to his speech as a model of reassurance and perseverance.

> *"Never give in, never give in, never, never, never, never—in nothing, great or small, large or petty — never give in except to convictions of honour and good sense. Never yield to force; never yield to the apparently overwhelming might of the enemy. We stood all alone a year ago, and to many countries it seemed that our account was closed, we were finished. All this tradition of ours, our songs, our School*

history, this part of the history of this country, were gone and finished and liquidated. Very different is the mood today. Britain, other nations thought, had drawn a sponge across her slate. But instead our country stood in the gap. There was no flinching and no thought of giving in; and by what seemed almost a miracle to those outside these Islands, though we ourselves never doubted it, we now find ourselves in a position where I say that we can be sure that we have only to persevere to conquer."

1. On a scale of 1 to 10, where is your focus?

2. Do you have a habit of multi-tasking during the day? In what ways can you minimize multitasking in order to improve your focus?

3. Are you an organized leader?

4. What coping strategies do you use to lower your stress level?

5. Are you taking strategic breaks throughout the day?

6. Do you pre-plan the evening before the next work day?

7. Where is your intensity? Are you a micromanager or a leader with relaxed intensity?

Chapter 3
Strategy Does Not Necessarily Equal Strong Tactics But Strong Tactics Can Equal A Great Strategy

"Without strategy execution is aimless. Without execution, strategy is useless."

— Morris Chang, founder and CEO of Taiwan Semiconductor Manufacturing Co.

STRATEGY

Although his job wasn't as an astronaut or a rocket scientist, the janitor at NASA understood strategy. While touring NASA for the first time, President John F. Kennedy asked him what he did there. The janitor replied, "I'm helping put a man on the moon." He had strategic vision. Some people do not understand the concept of strategy as well as the janitor understood it. They can have preconceived ideas that strategy is a plan on paper that ends up gathering dust or filed away to be quickly forgotten. It is easy to believe that as long as everyone in the company knows what they are doing and does their part, the company will run smoothly. However, leaders who understand the value of having a strategy will develop a plan to be exceptional at providing the correct product or service to their target customer.

When people think about strategy and tactics, oftentimes they envision war and war heroes. That is where we hear those terms mentioned the most, and we can learn a lot about them from war history. Before successful leaders in war and in business consider their tactics, they lay out a strategy. A common misconception is that strategy is competing to be the best in the growing of a company. To be clear, strategy is not about being the best; it is about being unique. It is not about growing a company; growth is the result of a strategy. It is about the direction an individual, a leader of a troop, or an organization intends to go.

Because having a sound strategy is crucial in war, there is an expression commander use to carry out their ultimate goal. It is known as the Commander's Intent. Every soldier knows that if they are unable to perform each task succinctly, the final strategy will be to follow the Commander's Intent. In the same way, a successful leader must communicate the direction of their organization so that everyone has a clear understanding of the desired outcome. Therefore, your tactical execution must have focus. Many leaders believe that focus must be on quality, innovation, profitability and growth. These four things depend on having strategy and execution blend flawlessly.

When applying strategies to industry, it is possible to have several companies succeeding the industry average. Each uses a different strategy; therefore, they do not pose a threat to one another. Because strategy is about being unique, you should never imitate your competition. Instead, work on making your company stand out. Unlike war, when referring to strategy, there can be many winners.

Julius Caesar is a prime example of a strategic leader. He is famous for the formation of armed legions, and he wrote many manuscripts about how to succeed in warfare. Most armies today copy many of his military maneuvers. Literally every day, his orders or remarks regarding military decisions are used. When he was told not to cross the Rubicon River into Italian territory, he said, "The die is cast," meaning he had already made the decision to cross it. Another quote, "Veni, Vidi, Vici (I came, I saw, I conquered)" is used often when someone has accomplished any kind of goal whether it be in business or a personal conquest.

"Strategy without tactics is the long road to victory. Tactics without strategy is the noise before defeat."

— Chinese Military Strategist, Sun Tzu

TACTICS

In as much as strategy is the plan to succeed, execution with carefully laid-out tactics is the implementation of the strategy. For years, studies have been done about the relationship between strategy and execution by Apple, Amazon, IKEA and other giants. Their secret for successful cohesion between strategy and execution is to fit the strategic into an everyday event. In other words, your strategy and execution must be closely linked by creating new, innovative entities that give your company a fresh look. This action must be consistent in every product and service your company has available. When working to reach a target market, tactics are the part of execution that is used to prevent your client from going to a competitor.

A high-octane leader understands that winning over a customer can be likened to being the winner in a motor racing competition. The drivers score points against the opposition. These points accrue over a season and determine the driver standings, as well as the owner standings. The way in which a driver scores points is through their maneuvers (tactics) on the racetrack. In referring to new technology being adopted by NASCAR, Emerson Fittipaldi, two-time winner of both the

Formula I World Championship and the Indy 500, said that overtaking another car is still difficult because it's supposed to be difficult. "That's what makes a great passing maneuver such a wonderful spectacle to behold."

For your tactics to be most effective, they must align with your strategy. The military has demonstrated both the identity and use of strategy and tactics. Military tactics are defined as "the techniques for using weapons or military units in combination for engagement and defeat of an enemy in battle." What are your techniques for achieving your strategy? What enemies do you need to defeat? It can be effective to give them or it a name. Sometimes the enemy is merely the fear of failure. In this regard, President Franklin Delano Roosevelt said, "We have nothing to fear but fear itself." Success in business, one battle at a time, can overcome the fear of failure.

In using the military to explain tactics, you can look to WWII to see the most brilliant war tacticians of the past century. Some would consider them tactical geniuses. The two standout generals in WWII were the United State's George S. Patton and Germany's Erwin Rommel. They fought some of the most pivotal battles in the war. They were always trying to guess the other's next move as they maneuvered their troops. General Patton mastered the Nazi's patented tactic called *Blitzcreig*. He took the Nazi's own tactic and used it to defeat them not only in North Africa but also in six other countries.

Patton's nemesis, Erwin Rommel, who was arguably the best tactician during World War II, was a lousy strategist. Although he was told not to cross into Egypt, he did so anyway which ended up being his most costly mistake. He faced a terrain where his flank tactics wouldn't work, and that resulted in his defeat. This demonstrates that even great tacticians can defeat themselves when strategy is forgotten on the road to success.

In order to avoid a Pyrrhic victory, high-octane leaders must learn from Pyrrhus and Rommel. The original Pyrrhic victory was led by Pyrrhus, King of Epirus, whose costly battles against the Romans depleted his resources. According to the historian, Plutarch, Pyrrhus muttered, "If we are victorious in one more battle with the Romans, we shall be utterly ruined." Rommel's defeat is referred to as a Pyrrhic victory because without a carefully planned out strategy, great tactics will not matter in the end. There have been many Pyrrhic victories, most notably the Battle of Bunker Hill and the Alamo. Therefore, as you analyze your tactics, you must ensure that you have a workable strategy. Otherwise, you will either be spinning your wheels or continually feeling defeated in your search for new ideas.

For the best results when implementing your strategy, it is wise to understand the type of leader that you are. Even though successful leaders share certain characteristics, they may have very different leadership styles. When looking at historical leaders such as General George S. Patton and Napoleon Bonaparte, you will notice that they were autocratic leaders. Some modern-day leaders in business such as Warren Buffet fall into the category of transformational leadership. Whichever category describes you, it is important to understand all of the leadership styles so that you can successfully work with leaders who are different from you. You must also consider that business models are constantly changing and that new generations who are entering the workplace require more flexibility from their leaders.

Successful leaders will adopt different leadership styles that align with the characteristics of their team. You should assess each situation in order to pivot when necessary to meet certain goals. For example, an employee who isn't very driven but is highly skilled will require the manager to have more of a creative leadership style – to be a motivator and an inspiration to the worker. Whereas the employee who isn't very skilled and also isn't driven will require a slightly different kind of manager – one who encourages yet demands quality work. You will identify with one leadership style more than another, but keep in mind that one style usually does not work for everyone. Start with these five leadership types and see which ones align with your present approach. Studying these will assist you in discovering or sharpening your own unique style.

THE VISIONARY LEADER

They are the entrepreneurs and the big dreamers. They do not follow conventional rules and are always looking for a better way to do things. They do not seek control and their desire is for those on their team to be free to be creative and innovative. These are big-picture people who daily work toward their vision. They are able to see future possibilities that others cannot see.

Example: Elon Musk of SpaceX and Tesla Motors – "We are going to land people on Mars by 2025."

THE TRANSFORMATIONAL LEADER

In order for people to become excellent transformational leaders, they must be able to be personally successful, influential, and teachable. This approach is for changing social systems and individuals. The goal is to develop followers into leaders.

Example: Andrew Carnegie, American steel magnate in the late 19th century – "No man will make a great leader who wants to do it all himself or get all the credit for doing it."

THE PACESETTER LEADER

They set the standard high for themselves and others around

them. They obsess about doing things better and faster. They are like the pace car in a motor car race which positions the racers in the warm-up before the actual race. The pace car also returns to the track to set things back in motion in the event of a disturbance or accident on the track.

Example: Steve Jobs, Apple co-founder and CEO – "Be a yardstick of quality. Some people aren't used to an environment where excellence is expected."

THE DEMOCRATIC LEADER

Also known as a participative leader, they believe there is room at the table for everyone regardless of job title or status. All opinions are of equal value and a decision is made after everyone has input. It is similar to the Visionary leader in that there is encouragement for the free expression of ideas.

Example: Indra Nooyi, CEO and Chairman of PepsiCo. – "I wouldn't ask anyone to do anything I wouldn't do myself."

THE AFFILIATIVE LEADER

Known for building teams that feel connected to each other. They are a master at building relationships. They are harmonious and help to solve conflicts. Leading by building strong emotional bonds, their team will stick by them through thick or thin. They create a familial type atmosphere in their organization.

Example: Joe Torre, Manager of the New York Yankees 1996 to 2007 – "Competing at the highest level is not about winning. It's about preparation, courage, understanding and nurturing your people, and heart. Winning is the outcome."

ADDITIVE #3
SELF-AWARENESS

"A good plan violently executed right now is far better than a perfect plan executed next week." – General George S. Patton

The answers to the following questions are the high-octane maintenance of your day-to-day strategy.

1. Where do I compete?
2. What unique value do I bring?
3. What resources and capabilities do I utilize to deliver my unique value?
4. How do I sustain my ability to provide that unique value?
5. What is my personal and company leadership strategy?
6. What tactics am I using to implement my strategy?
7. What is my leadership style; am I willing to adapt it to work well with my subordinates?

Chapter 4
Communication Must Be 360°

"I'm a great believer that any tool that enhances communication has profound effects in terms of how people can learn from each other, and how they can achieve the kind of freedoms that they're interested in." - Bill Gates, Co-founder of Microsoft Corporation

It always amazes me when I meet a couple who has been together for over 50 years. It is becoming a rarity; therefore, I feel compelled to ask them their secret. Of all of the couples that I have met over my lifetime, the overwhelming majority say that the secret to staying together as long as they have is by successfully communicating with one another. Lack of communication continually ranks in the top 3 of the top 10 reasons relationships do not succeed. In business, you will find the same scenario. Because organizations are based on relationships, whether they are internal or external, the success of that organization depends on a healthy climate of communication.

One way to create a positive working environment with healthy relationships is to make sure that communication is 360 degrees. In order to achieve this, a 360-degree assessment is commonly used to measure performance, personal growth and development – or a combination of the two. This system is used extensively in 85% of Fortune 500 companies as a central part of their leadership development procedures. 360-degree communication varies from company to company, but it is the entirety of communication – a complete circle of communication involving everyone. This strategy serves all parties associated with the organization: employees, management, shareholders, suppliers, and customers. Used successfully, the 360-degree assessment increases engagement, identifies training opportunities and helps employees develop in their own roles while eventually moving into leadership positions. Although it is about the entire organization, the following categories are focused on one at a time.

- Top level = client / executive
- Mid-level = peers / functional managers
- Subordinates = team members

Responsibilities vary from employee to employee; therefore, clients and shareholders will have different communication needs than functional managers or team members, as well as the different communication needs between suppliers and customers. Each group requires the appropriate form of information and the understanding of how to assimilate and implement that information.

It is also important for leaders like CEOs and upper management personnel to go through the program themselves. This way, they can relay a positive experience to other employees. Leaders set the example in any organization from taking on major projects externally to working to improve the company internally. Everyone can be better. No one has arrived at perfection yet. Ultimately, the goal is for employees to develop certain skills so they can move upward to succeed in a leadership role, eventually becoming a high-octane leader.

CORE COMPETENCIES

When beginning a 360-degree assessment, it is necessary to define the objective/s of the assessment. What is its purpose for your organization is a question that needs to be answered first. Generally, it is known as an excellent tool for measuring the core competencies employees need in order to succeed within an organization. Therefore, you must define your metrics to have acceptable results that will be useful for your company. In order for this to bear fruit, it is necessary to understand which competencies are important to the organization. Some of the metrics that have been successfully used to achieve 360 communication are:

- Teamwork
- Leadership
- Planning
- Attentiveness
- Positivity
- Work Ethic
- Listening
- Business Acumen

Additionally, it is optimal to give the 360-degree assessment separately in regard to performance and salary reviews. If used only as a developmental tool, it will limit exaggerated feedback. People often will give unrealistic responses or suggestions that do not benefit the employee or the organization. To avoid assessments that are geared towards undermining a coworker or pushing for a raise, using it as a separate developmental tool reduces the percentage of unhelpful commentary.

EXPECTATIONS

Theoretically, the 360-degree assessment tool sounds like a

perfect communication device. However, many individuals in the workplace have become anxious about participating in any type of personal data collection. In order to put workers at ease, every facet of the assessment they are asked to complete must be understood by them. It is important to start the process by explaining the expectations.

The employees should be informed as to whether it is a self-assessment or a peer-assessment. If you require them to perform a self-assessment, explain to them why this is important for both them and the company. It is essential to detail their responsibilities for participation in the process. Communicate the key time frames for completing certain sections, etc. Furthermore, they will need to know: why the data is being collected, how the data is going to be used, and what skills and attributes will be measured.

CONFIDENTIALITY

Knowing that the assessment will be administered confidentially will put employees at ease. This allows them to give the feedback that the company desires – honest, constructive feedback. Be sure to communicate to staff that only HR and the employee being evaluated will see the report.

In order to keep the identity of the reviewer private, it is essential that they understand not to include details that identify them or the recipient of the report. Here are a few examples of what not to write if the feedback is in text format.

- "In our meeting last Wednesday, he/she said…."
- "The review he/she had of my report on…."
- "While working on this project for him/her…."

There is always a potential violation of confidentiality that could result in the revelation of the reviewer's identity. In some cases, the reviewer does not mind being known – especially if they have worked well with one another for some time. One way to ensure confidentiality is by using an outside firm to administer the assessment electronically. There are many available on the market but do your research because some are better than others.

EFFECTIVENESS OF THE PLAN

Many organizations that implement the 360-degree communication approach rely on internal human resource coaches to assist their employees in understanding and implementing feedback. This should be a positive experience. Mandatory human resource participation in their own 360-degree assessment is necessary, so that they can positively convey how it has made them more productive in certain areas.

Employees can work with their coach in creating a personal action plan with steps to address any issues that need improvement. For example: When providing constructive feedback, it is necessary to put it in a positive light. Saying, "She is a terrible public speaker" isn't going to be as effective as, "If she focused on one-on-one communication with her staff, we would gain more from her directives." This can be a tragic setback if not done correctly. The latter is specific and focused on the area that needs work. Remember, motivation for improvement is the goal of 360-degree communication.

PROVIDING FEEDBACK

If an employee is distressed or concerned about their feedback, they will want an opportunity to discuss their results and reflect on their options for improvement. It has been noted that an internal coach is more effective with employees than an external coach. In working with upper management, an outside coach tends to be more effectual.

For those who take the time to provide feedback to their sub-ordinates or upper management, it is critical that they give feedback that is useful. In order for 360-degree communication to be practical, feedback should follow these guidelines.

- **Provide Main Points -** Focus on both the positive and negative aspects of your working relationship with your co-workers. Provide a maximum of 3 examples which is a number that most coaches and managers can effectively handle as well as the feedback from other employees.

- **Be Honest and Straightforward -** If you shield your words, you prevent your colleague from future growth in an area where they need improvement. You may be hindering your colleague's ability to advance to a particular position if you omit deserved criticism.

- **Provide Examples -** Providing examples is always an effective way to get your point across. You could say that your co-worker is not a good listener. However, if you were to provide an example, you might say that this particular employee tends to multi-task while talking to you, therefore, they miss half of what you are trying to communicate. Next, explain how this affects your productivity at work. This will help the human resources coach in using constructive criticism to provide the necessary steps for the employee to improve in this particular area.

- **Keep it Short and Simple -** The manager can deal with only a certain amount of information whether it is praiseworthy or disparaging. Make your key points as brief as you can. If you have criticisms, choose one to three to share. You don't need to include unnecessary details that don't clarify your key points. State the facts, as you see them. A manager will not enjoy dealing with a lot of trivial input.

• **Do not be Fearful of Repercussions -** There are many others providing feedback besides you. The upper management is looking for any negative patterns that they can discuss with the employee. The feedback from co-workers, the manager, and a self-evaluation are all factors in assisting with development, promotion or praise of the co-worker.

• **Reflect on Your Own Behavior -** As you rate your employee or manager, it is a perfect time to reflect on your actions in the workplace. It could be that the things that frustrate you about someone else, are the exact areas where you need improvement. This is why self-evaluation is so important.

ADDITIVE #4
COMPASSION/CONFIDENCE/COLLABORATION

"I think it's very important to have a feedback loop, where you're constantly thinking about what you've done and how you could be doing it better." — Elon Musk, CEO of SpaceX and Tesla Motors

A sample 360-degree feedback survey:

1. How effective is the employee's leadership style?
2. What do you like most about working with this employee?
3. How does the employee interact with others in the company?
4. What is the employee's commitment to company values?
5. Does the employee have the necessary skills for their particular job?
6. If you could make a suggestion regarding training topics for a particular employee, what might you suggest?
7. Do you struggle with some of the same areas as the employee you are evaluating?

Chapter 5
Momemtum Is Just As Important As Direction

"Business is like riding a bicycle. Either you keep moving or you fall down." – Frank Lloyd Wright, American architect, interior designer, writer and educator

MOMENTUM

W hen I was a child, I had fun occupying the driver's seat and pretending to drive my mom or dad's car. I could spend hours making "vroom" noises and weaving in and out of "traffic." I assume most of us did this as a child because during the mid-1940s, when my dad was very young, he was so poor that he would sit on a stump with a stick as his gear shift and drive his make-believe vehicle. For most kids, this type of pretend game was fun, but we had only imaginary momentum, and we knew we were going nowhere. In reality, anyone who pretends to drive an organization will soon be found out because of the lack of momentum. When an organization is not moving forward, it is like a parked car. It is not enough to be pointed in the right direction, because direction without momentum gets you nowhere. A high-octane leader knows how to generate momentum and keep it going.

It has been said that leaders create momentum, followers catch momentum, and managers continue the momentum. If leaders are looking for others to inspire them, then the organization is headed for trouble. They should model the kind of enthusiasm that motivates other people to continue to achieve. When you have momentum in business, everything naturally rolls forward: objectives are met, employees are proactive, customers are satisfied, and incredible results are produced. Momentum can induce rapid growth and propel your company toward its goals. These goals are reached by a continuum of achievements in rapid succession without cessation.

Just like a new outfit improves your outward appearance, momentum changes everyone's perspective of their leaders. People regard you as a genius and willingly look past your shortcomings. You are a shining star and can do no wrong. Like King Midas, everything you touch turns to gold. Your steady climb appears unwavering. While you accelerate with great momentum, you look better than you are, and you accomplish more than usual. As a result, many people and organizations will find security and value in associating with you.

You may look good only for a time however, unless you are able to sustain that forward motion. Momentum is variable and can change at a moment's notice, but the vision of an organization rarely changes. You do not have to look far to see that Toyota Motor Sales U.S.A., Inc. created a successful vision and sustains the momentum of that vision to this day. Their vision statement reads, "To be the most successful and respected car company in America." This vision represents the direction of the company. Toyota's vision has been successfully decomposed by the managers of the silos in the organization into operating standards. Those standards continue to be correctly driven down through the silos which render vision congruence or harmony. This congruence creates the momentum to accomplish the vision at Toyota and all other successful organizations.

Once you have achieved momentum like Toyota enjoys, it is up to you to sustain it. A great leader once said, "If you have momentum going, play the momentum." Everyone has seen companies who had great momentum lose it almost overnight. Statistics tell us that 80 % of businesses fail within the first 3 years. In 2017, Bed Bath and Beyond's Nasdaq momentum score of "F" showed that they had lost their momentum. They can come back, and they did to a certain degree, but their leaders must create that forward push and learn how to maintain it. The following suggestions are effective ways to keep the momentum that you create:

- **Play to Win –** If you change to a defensive strategy, you will lose the forward movement. When you play to win you remain on the offense. You stay positive which keeps company morale high.

- **Make Tough Choices –** Avoiding a decision does not avoid a bad outcome. Great leaders thrive on decision-making since they know it is critical to keep moving forward to stay ahead of the competition.

- **Understand the Customer Experience –** Experience what it is like to be a client or a customer of your business. Find out what their challenges are with your organization and repair any damage.

- **Welcome Change -** Do not fear change. Change is inevitable and usually profitable for an organization. You must keep progressing or prepare for disaster. The marketplace is competitive and changes from day to day.

DIRECTION

While momentum is absolutely essential for the success of any organization, it must be coupled with direction. Lewis Carroll, an English writer in the 1800s stated, "If you don't know where you are going, any road'll take you there." As a result, if you are not given direction, you will go any which way and so will everyone else in your company. But even if you have direction and are moving only at a snail's pace, your goals will not be achieved at a fast-enough rate. Owing to the fact that industry changes rapidly, your company would be left in the dust. Therefore, since the rate of change is accelerating, every team leader need to frequently clarify the vision of the company. In order for silos to work properly, congruent consistency is a must, or you will have hundreds of people in each silo going in hundreds of directions. High-octane leaders understand that momentum is just as important as direction. The following are fundamentals essential for leading with both.

- **Create a Vision –** The vision statement of an organization defines direction and focuses on what matters most. Many times, the vision statement is written on a prominent wall of the company to remind everyone there precisely why they are there. It is the aspirational focus of the future. It is a statement created by the leaders that tells the employees their designated destination. The vision must be articulated clearly to avoid misinterpretation. Knowing that a lack of vision is a road to nowhere, it asks: what are our dreams, what are we doing for the greater good, and who/what are we inspiring to change?

- **Possess a Mission -** The mission statement is the mechanics of how to realize the vision. It drives the company and enables everyone to stay focused. A strong mission statement also shapes the organization's culture. It asserts the questions: what do we do?, who are our clients/customers?, and how do we serve them?

• **Guide Behavior –** Giving orders does not encourage your team to do their best. Leaders demonstrate how to move forward by living the core values they expect from their team. Through these correct behaviors, they lead by example. This also allows the team to see the benefits of being consistent. Remember, good behavior is caught not taught.

• **Set Expectations –** It is important to describe the expectations and responsibilities for every employee. Understanding how to do their jobs satisfactorily not only contributes toward the vision but also to the outcomes needed for them and the company to succeed. As you set expectations you encourage personal development and create an environment of healthy competition.

• **Gauge Performance –** Leaders must be clear about performance. You should communicate goals and provide specific feedback. It is important to give accolades and reward integrity. This communicates to the team that they are going in the right direction. Always provide your team with a consistent message and the opportunity to address challenges. This type of leadership will create supporters throughout the organization.

ADDITIVE #5
VISIONARY

"Only those who will risk going too far can possibly find out how far one can go." - T. S. Eliot

1. Have you taken responsibility for the momentum in the area of which you are the leader?

2. How fast is your momentum?

3. Are you passionate about the vision?

4. Do you show enthusiasm for the vision at all times?

5. Are you consistent in demonstrating the core values of your organization?

6. Do you motivate others even when you don't feel like it?

7. Are you setting realistic expectations?

Chapter 6
Your Internal Script And Outward Behavior Must Be Congruent

"He who knows others is learned; He who knows himself is wise."— Lao-tzu, Tao te Ching

Have you ever been out shopping for a pre-owned vehicle and come upon one that has a flawless exterior? Every detail on the outside is amazing, but after you test-drive it, you find that nothing internally works right. As a result, the automobile is not considered a potential purchase. Likewise, the inner being of a successful leader, which reveals his character, will be the standard by which he is evaluated by other people. It is important to be genuine and to project that image.

Imagine that your daily work activities were secretly recorded, and you were able to watch and grade your leadership qualities at the end of each day. How would you rate your performance? Would you recognize yourself? Many times, we build ourselves up as someone we're not, but if we self-assess, we often find ourselves lacking in certain areas. High-octane leaders must critically analyze their personal lives in order to achieve optimal performance. Even though the goal of high octane leaders is not necessarily to please everyone, they must examine and know themselves in order to rectify the areas that need attention. This puts them on the right trajectory to achieve their goals.

Think of someone you know who a successful leader is. Do you possess similar qualities? Most people have encountered positive leadership models in their lives whether in a parent, a teacher, a coach, or a neighbor who has encouraged and expressed belief in them. Because of their influence, these mentors will always be fondly remembered because they made you feel more confident and capable. They are the high-octane leaders who encouraged you to believe in your own abilities and in turn positively affect countless others.

Very early in my career with my first real sales job, I had a sales manager who taught me quite a bit about selling, courage, and leadership. Most of his lessons occurred at 10 o'clock at night when I called him to tell him about my day. I had a young family and spent time playing with the kids, having dinner, putting the kids to bed, spending about an hour of downtime, then calling my sales manager to let him know about my day.

He was upbeat and enthusiastic and full of energy even though he was 30 years my senior. Our talks without fail specifically revolved around how to be a better salesperson and how to be a better person in general. I didn't know this at the time, but what I found out later was that when I called him at 10 o'clock at night he had already been in bed for an hour! Even though he was very tired from his day's work, he got up to take my call knowing my evening was busy with personal activity. That taught me something about leadership.

Because of that manager, I learned that leadership goes the extra mile. When a manager puts a lot of his free time into training you, he wants you to succeed and will take personal time to train and encourage you. Leadership qualities should soon be evident in your attitude and work ethic. As your work habits begin to mirror your mentor, you will be able to realize your growth as a leader. Taking a personal inventory will enable you to be the leader that you are meant to be. The following points present an impetus to evaluate your leadership performance.

Positive Thinking – There is a reason The Power of Positive Thinking by Norman Vincent Peale is one of the all-time most popular books on leadership qualities. He stated, "Have faith in your abilities! Without a humble but reasonable confidence in your own powers you cannot be successful or happy." Like a memorable melody, your attitude affects everyone around you. It transforms and motivates a team. Great leaders inspire others because they are inspired themselves. They look for the positive in every situation and in every person. Their optimism makes the workplace a happier place to be.

Stability/Consistency – Stability is something you may not think about as a leadership quality until it is absent. "The best managers in the world tend to be stable rather than excitable, consistent rather than erratic…" states Tomas Chamorro-Premuzic, a business psychologist in The Harvard Business Review. Stable leaders are like solid rock foundations. They are needed to build sound, foundational relationships. Conversely, some leaders who have unsound work habits are usually unstable and will not remain with the same company for very long. Consistency is the counterpart of stability. It is a well-traveled road with no unexpected turns. You can depend on that leader who always exhibits the same capable demeanor. An inconsistent leader can cause anxiety and discord in the workplace. In contrast to Steve Jobs, Sundar Pichai, Google's CEO, is highly successful because his co-workers find him predictable and humble. Despite being emotionally volatile, Jobs was very successful. He is an example of the exception rather than the rule.

Integrity – Leaders walk the talk – their deeds match their words. Integrity is defined as, "the quality of being honest and having strong principles, moral uprightness." If you were to explore the word integrity you would find that for years it has been ranked as one of the most important character traits of a respected leader. Like honesty, trust is a component of integrity. Trust is vital in all relationships. It is the glue that holds everything else together, whether in a business or any other kind of relationship.

Self-Motivated – Motivated leaders achieve beyond their own expectations and many times... everyone else's. Most people are motivated by external factors – impressive salaries and titles. How often have you heard, "Show me the money!" In contrast, those with leadership qualities are motivated by an intrinsic desire to see others achieve. Great leaders get results, whereas people with little motivation struggle in the role of leader. As a rule, people who are highly self-motivated remain optimistic even when the deck seems stacked against them. They continue to visualize their goals and find a way to reach them.

Visionary – Possessing a vision is the key to successfully leading others. Visionaries are able to see into the future and create a mental picture of what is to come. "Good business leaders create a vision, articulate the vision, passionately own the vision, and relentlessly drive it to completion." – Jack Welch, former chairman and CEO of General Electric. Seeing the big picture allows leaders to delegate the 80 % and focus on the vital 20%. As they communicate their vision to others, they plant the seeds of motivation to achieve that vision. Whatever you plant will grow and produce a million more seeds. A great example is McDonald's, the "burger joint," with restaurants throughout the world. It all started with one idea to sell ten-cent burgers and a refillable orange drink for a nickel.

Courteous – The corporate philosophy at Federal Express is "People-Service-Profit". They believe that if you take care of your employees, the employees will deliver a superior service which in turn makes their customer happy. A courteous leader is considerate of another people's time and knows how to manage their own. Being punctual is second nature. They are present in the moment. The cell phone is put away and you have their undivided attention. Albert Einstein, who was arguably the smartest man in the world, said, "I speak to everyone in the same way, whether he is the garbage man or the president of the university." It doesn't take a genius to understand that courtesy is necessary for ongoing success in any business.

HOW WILL OTHERS RATE YOUR PERFORMANCE?

In order to be a high-octane leader, you must see the picture other people see as they observe your actions. As outlined earlier, it is vital to have an accurate self-perception. What if the aforementioned scenario of rating your your personal performance involved both you and your co-workers reviewing your performance together. Could you handle the truth? Your co-workers observe your actions regularly and pass judgment on what you do, although you may never hear about it. So, the real question is: Should you ask them what they think?

High octane leader's welcome constructive criticism. They are the first ones to criticize themselves and to offer that same constructive criticism to others. When leaders are aware of their limitations, they are less likely to make mistakes that may cause their teams or organizations to fail. Those who have a false perception of themselves tend to rationalize their actions. They are defensive and use scapegoats for their failures. These are their common statements: "They don't really know me. I'm not that way. They are the ones who need to change." Deluded leaders are dangerous to the overall success of a company; their overconfidence puts their people at risk in the long run. Mistakes do happen. Being open with one another and forgiving unintentional errors is the correct reaction. Murphy's Law guarantees that things don't always run smoothly.

With most companies and corporations today, workplace surveys and questionnaires have been found to benefit their employees considerably. The following is a sample of a survey used to evaluate the leaders of an organization.

ADDITIVE #6
INTEGRITY

"The truth of the matter is that you always know the right thing to do. The hard part is doing it." – General H. Norman Schwarzkopf

Leadership Survey

1. Are you self-motivated?

2. Are you a trust-builder?

3. Do you inspire team members and work to build a strong team?

4. Do you introduce new ways of "thinking" and "doing"?

5. Are you an outstanding communicator, skilled at both listening and messaging?

6. Do you routinely provide feedback and coaching to their team?

7. Do you outstanding performance?

8. Are you consistently explaining complex concepts and teaching them to their team?

Chapter 7
Incremental Change Is As Important As Massive Disruption

"Great things are done by a series of small things brought together."
— Vincent Van Gogh

Change – some people welcome it; others try to delay it, but it is an inescapable part of life and business. It transitions us from one phase to the next. Specialists have divi – ded change into two broad categories: incremental change and massive disruption. It is important for an organization to be prepared for both. One of the secrets of high-octane leaders is that they embrace change as an inevitable factor in the life-cycle of any enterprise. They create a climate of adaptability in their organizations to respond to the opportunities that arise from each.

INCREMENTAL CHANGE

Most of the change that we experience every day is incremental change. Sometimes it is barely noticeable, but over time the slight improvements, such as cost reductions and upgrades to existing products, can clearly be realized. Also, It is more expedient than turning the whole establishment upside down as it makes use of your current technology in your current market. A software update is an example of how we are affected by incremental change every day in the workplace. The small changes are actually creative updates over a period of time that bring us value. Because it is a low risk option, it is the most popular form of change and a failsafe way to continue innovation and growth.

Almost all companies engage in incremental change in one form or another. One example is how Coca-Cola has kept a 130-year-old brand relevant. Over the years they have incrementally unveiled line extensions such as Vanilla Coke, Cherry Coke and Coke with Lime. But, more than thirty years ago mass hysteria broke out when Coca-Cola introduced a new soft drink called 'New Coke.' This new formula would save Coke about $50 million per year by cutting back on some of the costliest ingredients. Not a good idea! They were inundated with letters and phone messages from frenzied consumers demanding the return of their beloved soft drink-the REAL Coke. Less than three months later, the company brought back the original Coke – rebranding it as Coca-Cola Classic. This incident could have been their undoing! Nonetheless, as they continue to follow popular trends, they have been able to bring something new to their customers without damaging their brand as they almost did with 'New Coke' in 1985.

Although incremental change has been deemed the safer option in decision making, ironically it can also be the death knell to a company. For example, many years ago, Kodak was the leader in the photography industry which brought welcome changes in film to their customers. Unknown to the public, Kodak actually invented the first digital camera. However, the fear of damaging their film business caused them to hesitate in releasing this new technology to the marketplace. As they held back their technology, other companies developed similar technology with superior imaging, which made Kodak's technology obsolete. This incident caused a huge disruption in the Kodak organization.

It is critical that company leaders create a climate of adaptability in order for their employees to be prepared for incremental changes or massive disruption in their organizations. A shrewd leader should implement a change-management program for disruption occurrences. When you can determine the current state of your team, and where it needs to be when a disruption occurs, you can be adequately prepared for it. After considering the kinds of disruptors their organization will be able to control, high-octane leaders must assess how each of these factors might affect their organization.

- **Adequate staff** – Managers rely on their staff to ensure that change happens. Without enough workers, a company would have difficulty in managing an influx of brand new ideas and strategies.

- **Open communication** – Maintaining the momentum and keeping spirits high is critical. By frequently communicating with your managers, you ensure that they are all on the same page. They should feel secure in asking questions and discussing any information that they deem valuable.

- **Equip your managers** – Do your managers have the tools necessary to support major transitions in the company? They are the key translators from you to the team. It is critical that they understand and convey the message correctly and efficiently to the team members. They must understand their role during the company's transitions.

MASSIVE DISRUPTION

"Without change there is no innovation, creativity, or incentive for improvement. Those who initiate change will have a better opportunity to manage the change that is inevitable." — William Pollard

Ironically, massive disruption can be both creative and destructive. Sometimes a market can be massively disrupted when new ideas or products are introduced unexpectedly. Unfortunately, some organizations will be put out of business. Clayton Christensen, who coined a similar term, "disruptive innovation," defines it as "disrupting an existing market, industry, or technology to produce something new and more efficient and worthwhile." One such disruption was the App Store. Although Apple was not the first creator of apps, it reinvented a market when it launched its App Store in 2008 containing 500 apps. It had reportedly hit 2 million apps in early 2018. Other examples are the Smart Car and Amazon.

Massive disruption often depends on incremental improvements within the same field. Taxis and limousine companies have been around for almost a century providing transit to and from airports, around town, from city to city, etc. Over the years, they have improved their service to customers, but never in a big way. What a disruption it must have been when Uber was introduced! With their focus on convenience, the innovators of Uber have done exactly what disruptors are expected to do. Uber has brought change to the transit system by cornering a share of that business. Another company that did the same thing is Airbnb. Like Uber, with the focus on convenience and comfort, this hotel business came up with an online and mobile app for the general public and travelers, and unlike most hotels, imposed no restrictions which would turn away some clients. Both disruptors have benefited in a big way.

Entrepreneurs are born every day. Anyone with a great idea can become a success. Even though there are risks in starting a new business, it is the small companies or "new kids on the block" that normally bring about huge disruptions. These disruptors with an eye-catching idea are usually able to find their own niche instead of competing for a market share. And their huge, risky venture sometimes reaps dividends. Disruptors, like the Uber example, succeed in some fields exceptionally well while some companies who change incrementally, have slower, competitive growth.

Before you choose disruptive or incremental innovation, you must examine a few aspects of both kinds of change in regard to your organization. Although you may prefer one over the other, technological discoveries and inventions will determine your choice in some divisions. One division may thrive on disruptive changes while another may improve steadily with incremental changes. Basically, there is a place for both. It is important to research the rate of growth and the initiatives in each departmental division and determine the change which will meet the needs of each one. Small, incremental changes can be utilized in every division, affecting the existing products. New technology will determine disruptive change. Ultimately, utilization of both changes will result in stability in all divisions.

ADDITIVE #7
LIFE- LONG LEARNER

"The most difficult thing is the decision to act, the rest is merely tenacity. The fears are paper tigers. You can do anything you decide to do. You can act to change and control your life; and the procedure, the process is its own reward." – Amelia Earhart

1. How do you handle change?

2. Are you familiar with incremental change and massive disruption?

3. What incremental changes have you seen in your organization?

4. Does your organization have a climate of adaptability?

5. Do your managers feel sufficiently prepared if they were to experience massive disruption in the company?

6. Is there a balance of incremental change and massive disruption in your organization?

7. What is your transition plan for your team?

A Final Word

So, there you have it. I have attempted to put into words many ideas from business visionaries, leaders, philosophers, and authors throughout the ages who may have had something to say about leadership.

It is my hope that you can combine some of these bits and pieces into high-octane leadership ideas that will dictate future performance and allying your behaviors with an upward trajectory toward success.

If you would like to chat further feel free to set up a call with me. If this is for you or your small business, choose the first – GSC – option. If this is for your organization, choose the second – IDC option.

IMI
Intelligent Motivation Inc.

HOME   ABOUT   PROVOCATIVE LEADERSHIP   WHAT WE DO   MORE

SET UP A CALL WITH BILL

HOME // SET UP A CALL WITH BILL

Returning? Log In

Hello, I would love to talk with you about your goals and business needs! Just choose the time that works best for you.

I look forward to our dialouge...

Bill

1 Schedule Appointment

15 Minute Goal Setting Call (GSC) - The GSC is a no investment opportunity to discuss your personal goals and decide if one-on-one coaching is right for you.
15 minutes

Initial Discovery Call (IDC) - The IDC is an opportunity for you and I to get to know each other and assess if there is a natural fit between our organizations.
30 minutes

Provocative Leadership - Discovery Call. If you read the brochure, or watched the video and you want to know more about how Provocative Leadership can transform your life, then set up a no-obligation call now.
30 minutes

Public Speaking Call (PSC) - The PSC is designed to assist the individual in organization their thought and increasing the self confidence so that they can crush any presentation
30 minutes @ $150.00